counting in the garden

written by emily hruby

illustrated by patrick hruby

AMMO

This book is dedicated to our sister Bee
and to Mom, Dad, Jenny, and Zach

THERE ARE MANY WONDERFUL THINGS GROWING IN MY GARDEN.

I LIKE TO COUNT THEM...

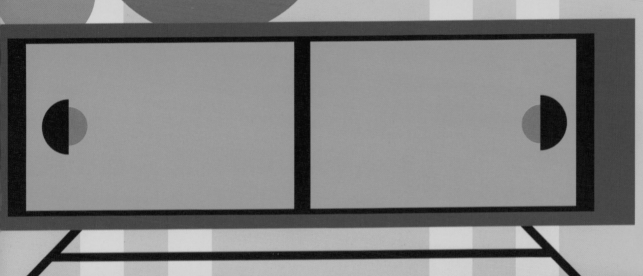

1 ONION, WITH MANY, MANY PEELS

2

TASTY TURNIPS, DEEP INSIDE THE GROUND

3

TINY THISTLES, THAT GREW BY ACCIDENT

4

FUN SUNFLOWERS, WITH VERY LONG STEMS

5
FRESH WATERMELONS, SHINY AND GREEN

6

SWEET STRAWBERRIES, HANGING FROM VINES

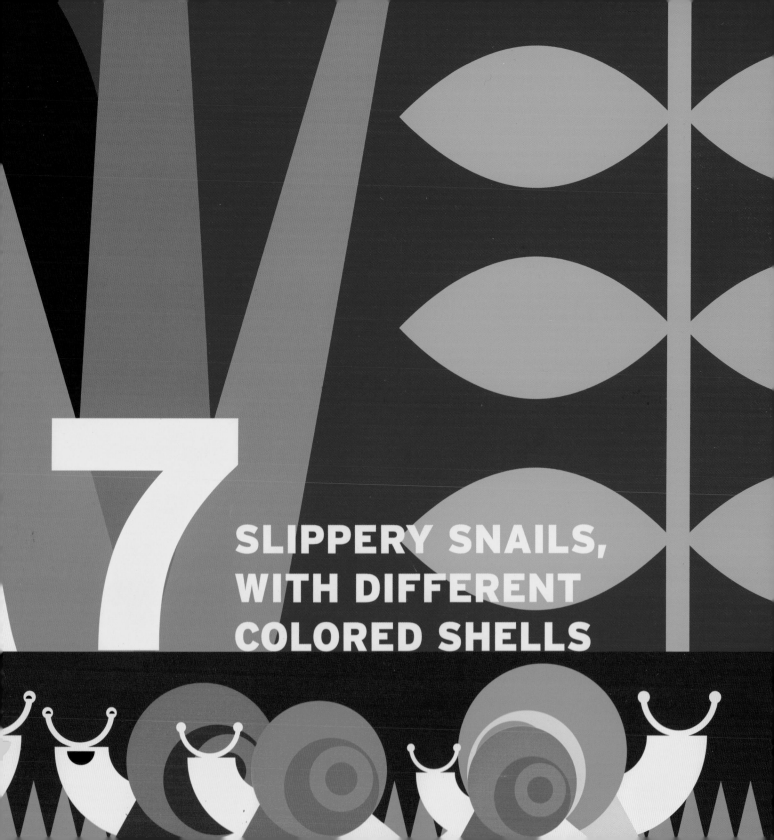

7
**SLIPPERY SNAILS,
WITH DIFFERENT
COLORED SHELLS**

8 EARTHWORMS, SQUIRMING THROUGH THE SOIL

9 NEW BUTTERFLIES, LEAVING THEIR COCOONS

10

**TENDER TOMATOES,
JUICY AND DELICIOUS!**

11

EASTER LILIES,
THAT OPEN LIKE
FIREWORKS

2 TALL TULIPS, IN A LONG YELLOW ROW

IT IS ALMOST TIME FOR LUNCH.

I THINK I WILL PICK THE TASTY THINGS FROM MY GARDEN TO EAT!

Art Direction: Gloria Fowler

For more children's books and products visit us at:
www.ammobooks.com